I0442208

From the Top: Shaping America's Arctic Policy and Strategy

I believe in the future he who holds Alaska will rule the world, and I think it is the most important strategic place in the world.

—Brigadier General Billy Mitchel l[1]

With his testimony to the 73rd United States Congress almost eighty years ago, air pioneer Billy Mitchell highlighted the strategic geographic significance of the Alaska Territory to future conflict. Historically, the United States government has ignored the importance of the Arctic and has been late to react to changes in the region. Today, unique geographic developments and adjustments in the international political landscape are highlighting the geopolitical importance of Alaska and the Arctic Region once again. Three distinct trends have contributed to renewed interest in the Arctic: new emerging sea lanes due to climate change, increased natural resource competition, and the rise of competitors in the region. This paper will examine the emergence of these trends and offer recommendations for strengthening current US Arctic policy and strategy.

Definitions and Methodology

Before one can say that Alaska or the Arctic is geopolitically important, a common understanding of the terms is useful. Saul Bernard Cohen defines *geopolitics* as an analytical mode "relating diversity in content and scale of geographical settings to exercise of political power."[2] In other words, geopolitics is the relationship between geography (land) and political power. For the purposes of this paper, *Alaska* will refer to the State of Alaska and the land within its legal borders. The Arctic Research and Policy Act of 1984 (ARPA) codifies the term *Arctic*:

> As used in this title, the term "Arctic" means all United States and foreign territory north of the Arctic Circle and all United States territory north and

west of the boundary formed by the Porcupine, Yukon, and Kuskokwim Rivers [in Alaska]; all contiguous seas, including the Arctic Ocean and the Beaufort, Bering, and Chukchi Seas; and the Aleutian chain.[3]

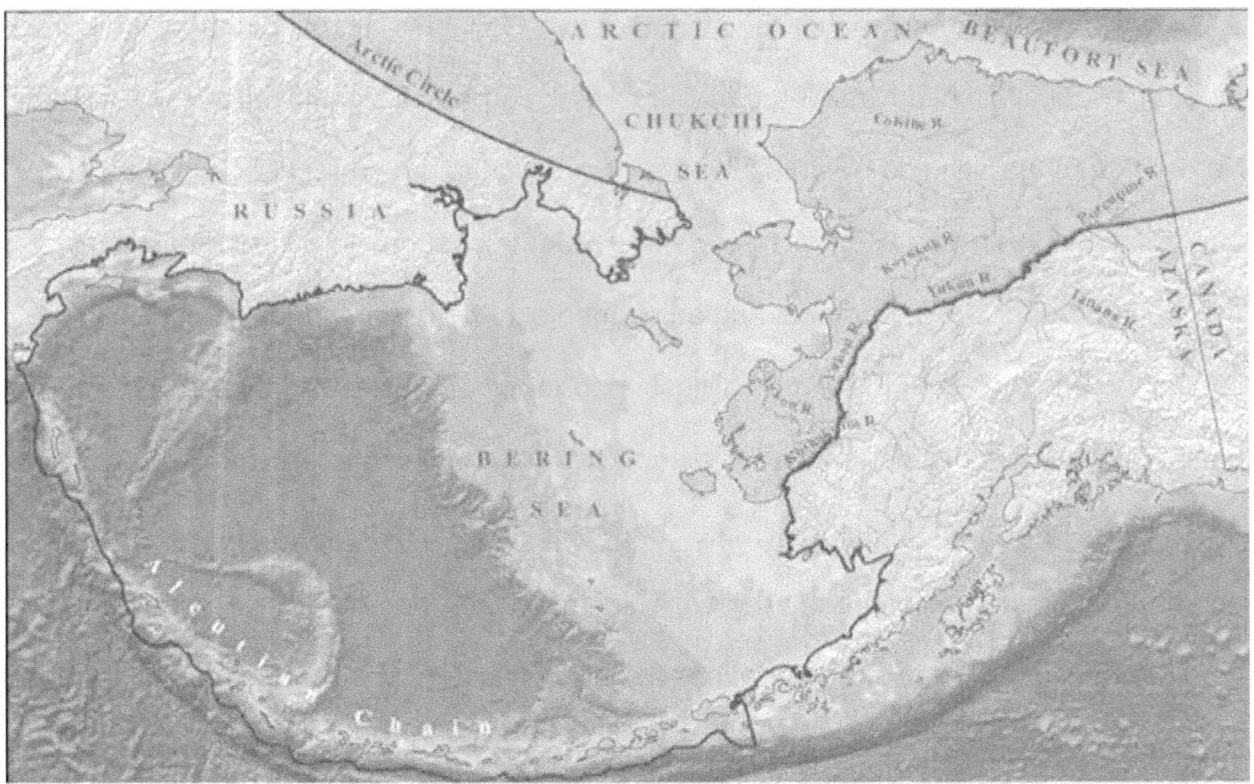

Figure 1. Map of Arctic per ARPA (outlined)

The categories of geography and political power and the interaction between them serve to illuminate both challenges and opportunities in the Arctic, and will frame an examination of the current trends.

Changing Geography

In the middle of the twentieth century, two students of geopolitics emerged who offered fundamental realizations about global geography and what it meant for the future. George Renner and Alexander DeSeversky were air power advocates who espoused a similar view of world geography and one that differed significantly from their contemporaries. Instead of looking at the world map from the perspective of the equator, they viewed the world from the North Pole.

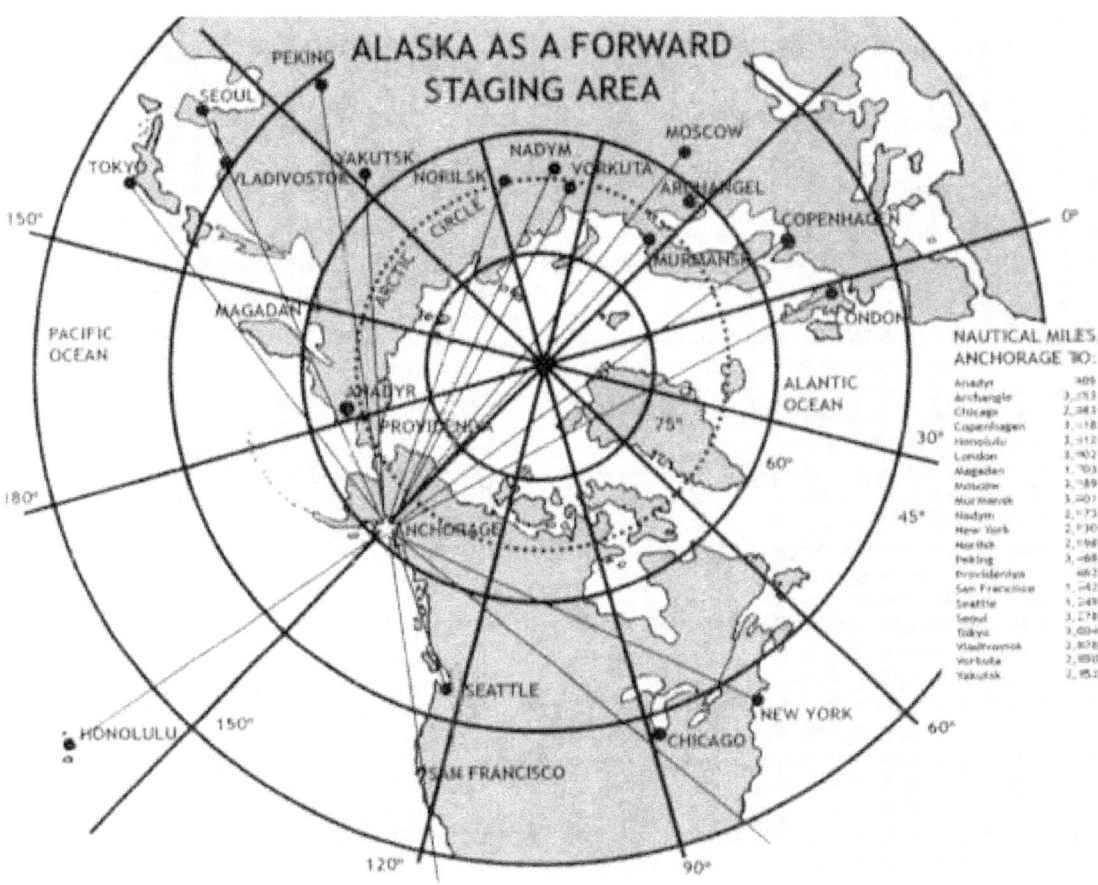

Figure 2. Northern Hemisphere Viewed from the North Pole[4]

Renner expanded on the theory of Halford Mackinder that posited control of the world was to be held by whoever controlled the great Eurasian heartland. Renner argued that air power, unconstrained by terrain or water, could connect the Eurasian heartland with a smaller heartland covering most of Canada and the United States via the polar region in the north. According to Renner, this new central area would have immense strategic value.[5] DeSeversky envisioned a great intercontinental air war between the Soviets and the United States. His theory agreed with Renner's view of looking at the world from the top. "In this aerial age we must get used to looking 'down' on our planet from the North Pole. The continents which seemed east and west of us really lie due north."[6] While a bit overstated in the early Cold War era in which it was written, DeSeversky's point was prescient and well-made considering what the future of power projection and aerial technology became.

To whichever world view one ascribes, it is the inclusion of the 49th state that labels the United States an Arctic nation with national interests in the Far North. From the beginning, Alaska's strategic importance has been hotly debated and in and a permanent state of flux. Following Secretary of State William H. Seward's agreement with Russia for the purchase of the Alaska territory, there was a vigorous debate in Congress regarding the appropriation of the agreed upon price. Detractors like Representative Benjamin F. Butler saw Alaska as a worthless arctic wasteland while proponents of the purchase, such as Representative Nathaniel Banks of Massachusetts, agreed with Seward's strategic assessment and believed that Alaska was the key to controlling the Pacific. Dubbed "Seward's Folly" by many of his naysayers, Seward's appropriation nonetheless was approved and Alaska became an official United States territory in 1867.[7] Although Seward believed Alaska was geopolitically important, others have not always shared his vision. From the purchase until World War II, Alaska was certainly not treated as strategically important. During this 70 year period, with the exception of two events: responding to the volatile environment in Alaska's panhandle during the Yukon Gold Rush, and the heightened tension of the Russo-Japanese War, the US government virtually ignored the area.[8]

The looming threat of Japanese imperialism in the years leading up to Pearl Harbor began to change that neglect.

Historians have often said that World War II was the single most important event to shape the modern era, and with regard to Alaska, that is certainly the case. Prompted by the Japanese declaration that it would no longer abide by the Washington Naval Treaty of 1922, Congress and the War Department began to take the threat of Japanese action in the Aleutians more seriously, at least in the abstract. Congress passed the National Defense Act of 1935 with the defense of Alaska included as a key consideration. Unfortunately, Congress failed to appropriate corresponding funds to support the strategy.[9] The legislative branch appeared content to wait for a more overt threat. Only after the Hitler-Stalin pact and the publishing of an article about the construction of Nazi-Soviet partnered bases in Siberia did a frightened Congress, on April 22, 1940, appropriate more than 350 million dollars for Alaskan defense construction in eighteen months.[10] For the first time, as the northern anchor of the Alaska-Hawaii-Panama Canal strategic triangle for hemispheric defense embodied in the vaunted Orange plans, Alaska would gain more significant military forces and infrastructure.[11]

Following the surprise attack on Pearl Harbor, the American military and the Japanese enemy were both quick to realize the strategic value of Alaska and its Aleutian Island chain to any prospective Pacific campaign. The Americans under the leadership of (then) Colonel Simon Bolivar Buckner, Commander of Alaska Defense Command, immediately prepared to defend against a possible Japanese invasion. Meanwhile, the Japanese prepared to strike the Aleutians. The Doolittle Raid directly shaped Japanese offensive intentions toward Alaska. Not knowing where the strike had originated, Japanese officials believed the bombers came from the Aleutian Island chain, a mere 650 miles from the Japanese base at Paramushiro in the Kurile Islands. Thus, when designing their "M I Operation" for Midway and the Aleutians, Japanese planners had two operational objectives: destruction of the Pacific fleet and protection of the northern flank of the Japanese homeland.[12] For the Americans, the Japanese presence inside American territory on Attu and Kiska demanded appropriate response. US forces did not fail in protecting national sovereignty, and ejected the Japanese in a bitter and bloody campaign. In all, more than half a million combatants from the opposing sides participated in the Aleutian campaign.[13]

Another way the US exploited the strategic advantage of the Alaska territory in World War II was the opening of sea and air lines of communication to the Soviet Union. War materiel valued at more than $11.28 billion dollars was shipped to the Soviets through the lend-lease program, an opportunity afforded by President Roosevelt and Congress through the Lend-Lease Act enacted 11 March 1941. A significant amount of this aid flowed through Alaska at places such as Ladd Field (now Fort Wainwright) in Fairbanks and Unimak Pass near Dutch Harbor. The statistic of nearly 8,000 aircraft shipped is staggering by itself.[14] This uninterrupted flow of equipment to the Soviets clearly impacted the outcome of the war in dramatic fashion.

It is also impossible to dispute the implications of geographic proximity. As the only campaign of World War II carried out on North American soil, had the Japanese held a more aggressive intent beyond the Aleutians, the Americans and Canadians could have been forced to focus on continental defense which had been a key concern of the US Army before the war.[15] Conversely, bases in Alaska and the Aleutians could have supported a northern Pacific axis of advance against the Japanese home islands had it been required by operational plans. While many historians deem the battles of the northern Pacific inconsequential to the outcome of the war, the precedent established for Alaskan continental defense and power projection are enduring. Alaska's close geographic position in relation to the Soviet Union would once again become critical during the Cold War.

As America and the Soviet Union challenged each other for world hegemony following World War II, Alaska again was the closest piece of sovereign United States soil to the enemy. Short distances between the two continents had many implications including making Alaska a prime location for watching and listening to Soviet military activities in Siberia, for power projection to Asia, for bomber intercept, and missile defense activities. Not only was it easier to detect planes or missiles inbound to the continental US from the northern regions, northwest Alaska allowed seismic monitoring of Soviet nuclear programs and testing in Siberia. Additionally, while preparing for a potential war with the Soviets, Alaska provided a home field where the military might train and research equipment needs and capabilities in a cold weather environment on similar terrain. The military forces doing this monitoring, training, and preparing to project power required command and control. Alaska's two largest cities, Anchorage and Fairbanks, were ideally suited as headquarters locations.[16] Lastly, Alaska "possessed ten of the sixteen minerals crucial to the creation of Cold War industrial and military products."[17] As technology developed rapidly in this period, the significance of this mineral wealth should not be understated, and the existence of these valuable resources foreshadowed future resource competition in the region.

Recalling the airpower theorists, Alaska's central location allows quick access to all of the continents in the northern hemisphere. Alaskan seaports and airfields are ideally located for worldwide power projection. Maintaining a power projection capability in close geographic proximity to the Soviet threat clearly drove the DoD's investment and focus on Alaska during the Cold War. In fact, the military employed more people in Alaska, and spent more money than any other employer in the state until oil began to flow from the region in 1977.[18]

As demonstrated by the historical background, geography has shaped previous periods of focus on Alaska and the Arctic. Normally, one thinks of physical geography as remaining constant since large geographic changes are hard to notice in the span of one human lifetime. However, there is a dramatic contemporary change literally shifting the physical geography in the Arctic region. Although greater global warming and the long-term implications of such a development are still the topic of some debate, the onslaught of climate change in the form of melting Arctic sea ice is undeniable. "Because of climate change, the Arctic Ocean's summer ice cover is now half of what it was 50 years ago."[19] What may be more alarming, or encouraging depending on one's perspective, is the rate of sea ice loss. The frequency with which the "new low" for summer ice coverage occurs, and the magnitude of the loss, is increasing. For example, 2007 was the new low for summer ice coverage since records have been kept, and 2012 was lower yet.[20] Loss of sea ice has many implications for government, but a few focus areas for national security are the potential of newly opening sea lanes, increased human activity in the region as a result of increased access, and complication of homeland security and homeland defense.

In the past, the vast sheet of ice across the North Pole and the entire Arctic Region provided a sense of security with an actual physical barrier on the northern edge of North America. As demonstrated by the Cold War discussion, the major threat from the north was missile or airplane attack. An open sea line of communication onto the northern coast of Alaska could present massive new challenges for homeland defense These challenges to hemispheric security and homeland defense may require new basing or capabilities. However, this new open water also presents significant opportunities, including shorter transit times and increased access to natural resources lying beneath the seas.

Many early explorers searched for new western routes to Asia, and the Northwest Passage (north of Canada) and the Northeast Passage or Northern Sea Route (north of Russia) present two new alternatives. In the summer of 2007, thawing occurred of "the northern segment of the Northwest Passage across McClure Strait, offering a deep draft passage for the first time in history."[21] These new routes seem to offer dramatic savings opportunities for international shipping companies. The potential distance reduction (and thus, transit time) from Rotterdam to Yokohama, through the Northeast Passage, is more than a third of the current total. However, there are still challenges to be solved before a large increase in point to point shipping can be realized. First, while the northern straits are certainly opening for periods of time heretofore unseen, the exact time they will open and remain so is uncertain. Also, these newly opened waters still have floating pieces of ice, known as growlers, moving freely throughout the passages which means that ships cannot maintain the same speed navigating Arctic waters as in more temperate ones. This reduction in speed that offsets shorter distances, higher insurance fees, and additional equipment costs necessitated by transit through Arctic waters makes any near-term sustainable increase in long-haul transit problematic. More certain is that increased shipping activity in the region will be "destinational," driven by the thriving competition for natural resources.[22]

Since the 1977 opening of the Alaska Pipeline, America has recognized the value of Alaska's vast oil resources. With the melting Arctic sea ice and resultant access to the northern Bering and Chukchi Seas (north of Alaska) oil industry focus worldwide has turned from land-based oilfields on Alaska's North Slope to resources under the adjacent seas. In a 2008 report, the United States Geological Survey estimated that "90 billion barrels of oil, 1,669 trillion cubic feet of natural gas, and 44 billion barrels of natural gas liquids may remain to be found in the Arctic, of which approximately 84 percent is expected to occur in offshore areas."[23] This volume is staggering and roughly equal to15 percent of the world's undiscovered oil reserves and 30 percent of the undiscovered natural gas reserves. Oil companies are desperately seeking to lease mineral rights in the region. Royal Dutch Shell, for example, has been granted permission by the US Department of Interior and is scheduled to begin exploratory drilling in the Chukchi Sea this year. US companies are not alone in launching efforts to exploit these vast resources. Friends and rivals alike are granting permits to multi-national corporations to harvest oil and gas from their Arctic waters. Canada and Russia both have drilling and development projects underway.[24] It is not difficult to see the potential for contested waters and rights in the region with the increased human activity brought by this high level of mineral wealth. Contested waters bring major national security implications to the maritime domain that must be addressed quickly. Increased access and activity will require equipment that can break through ice and operate in extreme temperatures. However, geographic changes in the Arctic driven by climate change are only half the equation.

International Political Developments

The historical discussion demonstrated that the United States has been habitually slow to resource the region until a corresponding threat develops. The reemergence of Russia as a rival in the Arctic, and China's exponential economic growth and massive military buildup in the Asia-Pacific both represent significant challenges for the United States. Alaska is ideally positioned to influence action in both the Arctic and the Pacific.

In the post Cold-War era, all efforts to take advantage of the resources offered by new access in the Arctic should be cooperative and peaceful. History has shown us however, that economic interests of nation states often become flashpoints for renewed conflict. In August 2007, Russian explorer Arthur Chilingarov planted a Russian flag on the sea floor underneath the ice at the North Pole sparking astonishment and chagrin among the other Arctic nations. With Vladimir Putin back in power in Russia it is difficult to be certain that there is no nefarious intent in this antiquated but symbolic gesture. Since the post Cold War Russia has been unable to compete with the United States militarily, and Russia still desires to play the role of a global power, it has chosen to leverage its energy resources to balance western influence. Now, in separate policy pronouncements over the last four years, including its national security strategy, the

Russians have espoused the use of military force if faced with energy access problems in the Arctic and have pledged to bolster their border and security forces.[25]

Russia's security strategy and its diplomatic behavior are completely divergent with regard to the Arctic. Despite the ominous indicators on the security side, the Russian diplomatic approach is one of cooperation and international interaction. Russia has been a productive member of the Arctic Council, has worked with Norway to resolve boundary disputes in the Barents Sea, and even entered into economic agreements with the United States.[26] A recent agreement between ExxonMobil and the Russian energy giant Rosneft on exploration of Arctic energy resources is a positive sign.[27] Policymakers are unsure what circumstances might arise to swing the more docile Arctic diplomatic policy toward the more confrontational language by Russian national security practitioners. In the words of Secretary of State Hillary Clinton, "I think we just have to wait and see what the real objectives of the new Russian leadership are."[28]

Non-Arctic powers are also exploring their options in the region, raising some concern. The most significant example of this being China's newfound interest in the Arctic. Chinese companies recently have been exploring investment opportunities in Iceland. Also, "China has an unusually large embassy in Iceland and an Arctic science center on Norway's Svalbard Archipelago."[29] Is China attempting to get a foot in the Arctic door? Considering China's meteoric rise in economic strength and unprecedented military spending, any initiative outside its traditional area of influence is notable. The addition of non-Arctic players may significantly complicate diplomacy in the region, may increase the opportunity for unintended consequences, or may escalate a minor conflict between peripheral parties into a conflict between major powers.

Combined, the competition for natural resources made more accessible by climate change and the political developments in the Arctic and the Pacific create a significant challenge for US policymakers charged with protecting national interests. The policies and strategies the US government chooses to handle the increased human activity in the region and protect access to its resources will largely determine whether the Arctic continues as a region of cooperation or becomes a zone of conflict.

Current Policy and Strategy

Any discussion of national security interests should begin with the National Security Strategy (NSS) which, despite the title, is really the overarching national security policy document of the United States. The *National Security Strategy* dated May 2010, identifies four enduring national interests: security, prosperity, values and international order.[30] Current Arctic Policy, established by National Security Presidential Directive-66 (NSPD-66) signed by President George W. Bush, January 9, 2009, recognizes changing defense and homeland security requirements and increased human activity in the Arctic as a result of climate change as policy drivers. The policy identifies the United States as an "Arctic Nation" and lays out six compelling policy objectives in the Arctic:

- Meet national security and homeland security needs relevant to the Arctic region;

- Protect the Arctic environment and conserve its biological resources;

- Ensure that natural resource management and economic development in the region are environmentally sustainable;

- Strengthen institutions for cooperation among the eight Arctic nations (the United States, Canada, Denmark, Finland, Iceland, Norway, the Russian Federation, and Sweden);

- Involve the Arctic's indigenous communities in decisions that affect them; and

- Enhance scientific monitoring and research into local, regional, and global environmental issues.[31]

The current administration has not created a new Arctic Policy since taking office in 2009, but senior officials including Secretary Clinton have identified the Arctic as a region of "intense interest."[32] Additionally, there has been no significant action to resource a strategy to achieve Arctic policy objectives because policymakers have been focused on wars in the Middle East.

Coexisting with NSPD-66 and announced in January of 2012, is new strategic guidance for the Department of Defense (DoD). Entitled *Sustaining U.S. Global Leadership: Priorities for 21st Century Defense,* the document outlines a new focus on the Asia-Pacific region as the military exits from the wars in Iraq and Afghanistan and begins to face the realities of extreme fiscal constraints. Supporting the policy change in a recent speech to the Australian Parliament, President Obama stated, "…reductions in U. S. defense spending will not—I repeat, will not—come at the expense of the Asia Pacific."[33]

The Quadrennial Defense Review (QDR) 2010 also assigned four objectives for the DoD as it balances the risk to mission accomplishment with constrained resources. These objectives are:

- Prevail in today's wars

- Prevent and deter conflict

- Prepare to defeat adversaries and succeed in a wide range of contingencies

- Preserve and enhance the All-Volunteer Force.[34]

In its May 2011 report to Congress on Arctic operations, the DoD further distilled the six policy objectives from NSPD-66 and the four priorities from the QDR down to two primary objectives for the DoD in the Arctic region:

- Prevent and deter conflict in the Arctic

- Prepare to respond to a wide range of challenges and contingencies—operating in conjunction with other states when possible, and independently if necessary.

In addition, the strategic end state for the Arctic is defined as, "a stable and secure region where U.S. national interests are safeguarded and the U.S. homeland is protected."[35] With national interests at stake and new policy objectives (ends) established, an understanding of ways and means will assist in defining a strategy. The four elements of national power (diplomatic, informational, military, and economic) provide broad categories of ways to employ a range of resources available to implement national strategy.

NSPD-66 endows a strategy characterized by diplomatic primacy towards the Arctic and there are several key considerations for the diplomatic element. First, one must consider treaties and conventions. NSPD-66 states that no overarching international agreement, like the Antarctica Treaty, is necessary in the Arctic due to different "geopolitical circumstances."[36] Five states have Arctic coastlines and waters, and as a result have legitimate claims to natural resources located there. This is a major difference from Antarctica and justifies the policy statement.

The United Nations Convention on Law of the Sea (UNCLOS) is another convention that provides nation states the diplomatic means for claiming natural resources in the waters adjacent to their lands. UNCLOS defines the limits of international waters, economic exclusion zones, and the requirements for extending the continental shelf. UNCLOS serves as both an obstacle and an opportunity for US strategy in the Arctic. Although UNCLOS is largely consistent with other international norms and laws and the US generally abides by its provisions, the United States Senate has failed to ratify the convention. In May 2009, visiting fellow at the Council on Foreign Relations, Scott G. Borgerson, summed the implications up perfectly saying:

> By not joining, the United States is actually giving up sovereign rights---missing an opportunity for international recognition or massive expansion of U.S. resources jurisdiction over as much as one million square kilometers of ocean, an area half the size of the Louisiana Purchase. Remaining outside the convention prevents the United States from participating in the process of overseeing the claims of other countries to the extended continental shelf and from formally making its own.[37]

The US has unresolved maritime boundary disputes with Canada and Russia in the Chukchi and Bering Seas respectively. Although an agreement with Russia has been reached, the treaty has never been ratified by Russia. The Canadian dispute is ongoing.

The Department of State (DoS) is assigned as the lead executive department for participation in the Arctic Council. "The Arctic Council is a high-level intergovernmental forum to promote cooperation, coordination and interaction among the Arctic states."[38] There are eight members of the Arctic Council (Sweden, Denmark, Norway, Finland, Iceland, Canada, Russia, and the United States). The Arctic Council, while not regulatory or focused on defense issues, has been effective at building consensus on issues such as the environment and search and rescue cooperation.

16

Militarily, the United States faces numerous challenges in Arctic ways and means, but most fall under two categories: unity of command/legal authorities and maritime capabilities. The strategic document that assigns geographic territory and responsibilities to each of the Combatant Commands is the Department of Defense's *Unified Command Plan.* The current version (April 2011) firmly placed Alaska in US Northern Command (NORTHCOM) and charged the NORTHCOM Commander with advocating for Arctic capabilities.[39] Joint Task Force-Alaska (JTF-AK), a provisional headquarters reporting to NORTHCOM, exists for homeland defense and Defense Support of Civil Authorities (DSCA) missions. Complicating matters, the separate Alaskan Command (ALCOM), remains a sub-unified command of PACOM and retains operational control of Alaska-based military forces. Fortunately, there is an agreement between the two combatant commands that allows ALCOM to man JTF-AK. However, this remains a significant challenge to unity of command in pursuit of US interests in the Arctic.[40]

The Arctic is primarily a maritime environment that includes the homeland (State of Alaska) and its approaches. These characteristics of the operational environment make the United States Coast Guard (USCG) one of the most capable and well-positioned federal entities to influence Arctic strategy. However, according to USCG Commandant, Admiral Robert J. Papp, Jr., "the Arctic is emerging as the new maritime frontier, and the Coast Guard is challenged in responding to the current and emerging demands."[41] Ironically, although the Coast Guard Commandant says his service is challenged, the USCG employs the *only* operational icebreaker owned by the US, which places the country at a distinct disadvantage when compared with other Arctic nations.

Synchronized efforts between the USCG, belonging to the Department of Homeland Security (DHS), and the DoD will be imperative when deciphering both legal authority issues and capability requirements.

In order to achieve the end state articulated in the QDR, the DoD has devised Arctic Mission Areas, and conducted capabilities based assessments on the ability to perform those missions in the out years. Significant shortfalls exist in several areas including: ice and weather reporting; limited intelligence, surveillance and reconnaissance assets and capabilities; lack of ice capable vessels (neither icebreakers nor ice strengthened); and deep water port infrastructure. Despite these shortages, DoD asserts that it can meet all missions with current threats, conditions and capabilities, and that monitoring the situation in the Arctic and reacting with the right capabilities commensurate with the pace of opening of the region will suffice.[42]

The Arctic is currently out of the American public's spotlight, and thus, strategic messaging about the Arctic is meager. However, there are many audiences to address with strategic information themes. Currently, US actions speak clearly: the US is lagging behind other Arctic nations in both security preparations and claims to the continental shelf. This appearance must certainly be an encouraging sign to potential adversaries, and of concern to stakeholders and partners.

The long delay in ratification of UNCLOS is hampering economic claims to greater resources through the international process. Canada, Russia, and Norway are already aggressively pursuing exploitation of natural resources under the Arctic seas, as the US lags behind. NSPD-66's balance between energy and environment needs to be realized. Energy security is a key consideration for future national security and should not be delayed while competitors are hard at work.

Recommendations

With the increased importance of protecting US interests in the Arctic, a comprehensive US national strategy with proper identification of ends, ways and means will assist in keeping the Arctic region one of cooperation. The President should direct the Arctic Interagency Planning Council (AIPC) to undertake a holistic review of NSPD-66 validating or modifying Arctic policy objectives. Arctic objectives must be coherent and complementary to Asia-Pacific objectives, since many of the ways and means utilized to achieve these objectives will be shared between theaters. Detailed synchronization will enable success and assist with meeting fiscal realities because capabilities may be dual-purposed between executive departments or employed by multiple combatant commands. The complex division of responsibilities between DHS and DoD, and each departments corresponding level of effort in the Arctic must be articulated. Following the identification of a clear strategy to pursue validated Arctic objectives, actions must be directed and resourced under each element of national power.

Diplomatically, there are some low cost options for improving the stability and outlook in the Arctic. As a staunch proponent of maintaining freedom of navigation, the administration must deliberately facilitate the United States Senate's ratification of UNCLOS. Becoming a party to the convention will enable extension of the continental shelf thereby establishing and protecting US claims on resources, and discouraging claims on US sovereign resources by other states. DoS must develop detailed objectives for the American chairmanship of the Arctic Council following Canada's term.

Sweden did an admirable job of laying out initiatives during its chairmanship rotation and had great success.[43] Arctic Council leadership is a unique opportunity to further demonstrate to the international community that the United States can operate in an environment of collaboration and cooperation, without invoking its might as a superpower. DoS should also work to resolve our maritime boundary disputes with Russia and Canada by pursuing ratification and negotiation respectively. Arms control is important to the Russians, so perhaps tying any future agreements to the ratification of the border treaty would force closure to the issue. Lastly, diplomats should develop agreements with Arctic partners for the provision of complementary capabilities, such as icebreakers, during contingencies. These agreements may be in a multi-lateral forum such as the Arctic Council, or in the case of continental defense may be bi-lateral agreements with Canada. Military to military contacts may also be valuable in determining which capabilities each partner is able to provide.

In strategy documents, DoD has done an admirable job identifying required capabilities, but in reality has been less anxious to pursue procurement in this resource constrained environment. The tendency to wish away capability gaps by *relying on foreign partners* and/or *continuing to monitor* threats to US interests is prevalent. Partnering and waiting are approaches that do not support the DoD's ability to act independently or respond to a wide range of contingencies in a timely manner in accordance with the department's own objectives.[44] With long lead times for research, development, acquisition, and construction, these approaches to strategy carry considerable risk.

DoD must also address the command and control challenge between the sub-unified command, ALCOM and Joint Task Force-Alaska. Ohotnicky et al make a compelling argument and a sound recommendation for the dissolution of JTF-AK and transfer of ALCOM to NORTHCOM in their recent *Joint Forces Quarterly* article. Doing so would provide NORTHCOM a sub-unified command to focus on Arctic capabilities in accordance with the Unified Command Plan.[45] DoD must also examine allocation of forces that are located in Alaska. These units are needed for the PACOM Commander's contingency and theater engagement plans, but also must be able to perform contingency duties in the Arctic as human activity increases. In the sparsely populated reaches, sometimes the only response capability will belong to DoD and a mechanism for implementing such a response must be in place. Thus, both NORTHCOM and PACOM should advocate for Alaska basing for any units returned from Europe or rebased from CONUS to support the Pacific pivot. Dual apportionment is not new, but all parties must understand where the forces belong, and under what circumstances, in order to properly allocate mission oriented training opportunities and facilitate concurrent planning for both PACOM and NORTHCOM missions.

Arctic military capability focus should be on three maritime areas initially: maritime domain awareness (MDA), port facilities, and icebreakers. MDA can be facilitated by improving the communications architecture, enabling GPS signals that will work reliably in the northern latitudes, and developing Arctic capable Intelligence, Surveillance, and Reconnaissance (ISR) platforms that can survive the severe environmental conditions.[46] Both facility development and shipbuilding (icebreakers) require long-term planning and funding. In order to avoid the risk of being late to the fight with these capabilities, funding for research, development, and acquisition should be appropriated now. USCG and the United States Navy must collaborate to develop icebreaking and ice strengthened hulls and decide which entity will perform which tasks. Perhaps USCG handles icebreaking and surface patrols and USN handles sub-surface missions in the near-term, with an event oriented transition should a major contingency arise. In the meantime, DoD must work military-to-military contacts with partner nations such as Canada for sharing of icebreaking capabilities until procurement of additional assets can be completed. Lastly, the military must work with the AIPC to determine if new continental *land* defensive capabilities are required as a new *assailable* coast emerges on Alaska's North Slope.

Information operations should be explicitly synchronized with the other elements of national power. Audiences such as indigenous peoples, environmental groups, multi-national corporations, Arctic partners and potential adversaries must all receive messages. The primary medium however is *action*. By demonstrating focus on the changes in the Arctic region, and by acting responsibly to develop capabilities and resources, the US will demonstrate a desire to work peacefully in the region and demonstrate firm resolve to protect sovereignty and national interests. Those are great message themes to reinforce.

UNCLOS will aid the economic arm of Arctic power, but diplomatic settlement of boundary disputes is equally crucial. The US should also initiate deliberate development operations for new sources of oil and natural gas, which could dramatically shift US dependence on imports. A clear path and incentives for companies to obtain leases and licenses must be promoted in order to encourage further private investment.

Balance must be attained between environmental concerns and the advantages offered by new sources of energy.

Conclusion

Although the Arctic finds itself at the nexus of national security strategy once again, the current fiscal environment and the lack of perceived threat is significantly constraining preparation for future contingencies. The current approach of "wait and partner" entails significant risk that the US will not gain required capabilities in time to respond. A whole of government approach should be developed that is focused on a complementary strategy of using limited resources (means) in creative ways that ensure success in both the Pacific and the Arctic. Alaska, as the swinging door between the two areas of responsibility, is the perfect choice for basing of critical capabilities for both PACOM and NORTHCOM. As evidenced by history and through air power theory, the US is more than capable of projecting power from the 49th state. Integration of the DHS and the USCG into all Arctic planning is also imperative. The Coast Guard has the legal authority for homeland security, regional expertise, and most viable capability to operate in the Arctic maritime environment *today*. Military focus on awareness, integrated command and control, and facilities infrastructure for the Arctic maritime environment will allow DoD and DHS to combine coherent response and defense capabilities. The rationale for a comprehensive policy review and synchronization of ways and means offered here is a starting point for a more robust national strategy on the reemerging northern front.

Endnotes

[1] William Mitchell testimony, *Hearings before the Committee on Military Affairs*, February 13, 1935, 113-21, quoted in Galen Roger Perras, *Stepping Stones to Nowhere: The Aleutian*

Islands, Alaska, and the American Military Strategy, 1867-1945 (Annapolis, MD: Naval Institute Press, 2003), 30.

[2] Saul Bernard Cohen, *Geopolitics of the World System* (Lanham, MD: Rowman and Littlefield, 2003) 12.

[3] Ronald O'Rourke, *Changes in the Arctic: Background and Issues for Congress* (Washington, DC: U.S. Library of Congress, Congressional Research Service, January 2, 2013), 1.

[4] Laurel J. Hummel, "The U.S. Military as Geographical Agent: The Case of Cold War Alaska," *Geographical Review* 95, no.1 (January 2005): 49. Adapted from Cloe 1984. Cartography by Robert A. Getz, U.S. Military Academy.

[5] George T. Renner, *Human Geography in the Air Age* (New York, NY: Macmillan, 1942), 152.

[6] Alexander P. DeSeversky, *Air Power: Key to Survival* (New York, NY: Simon and Schuster, 1950) map insert.

[7] Perras, *Stepping Stones to Nowhere,* 6.

[8] Ibid, 6-8.

[9] Ibid, 30.

[10] Brian Garfield, *The Thousand Mile War: World War II in Alaska and the Aleutians* (Fairbanks, AK: The University of Alaska Press, 1969), 62.

[11] Ibid, 57.

[12] Ibid, 7.

[13] Jonathan M. Nielson, *Armed Forces on a Northern Frontier: The Military in Alaska's History, 1867-1987* (Westport, CT: Greenwood Press, 1988), 166.

[14] Ibid, 135-136.

[15] Ibid, 98.

[16] Hummel, "The U.S. Military," 48-53.

[17] Ibid, 48-49.

[18] Ibid, 58.

[19] Lawson W. Brigham, "Think Again: The Arctic," *Foreign Policy,* no.181 (Sept/Oct 2010): 72.

[20] For detailed data on snow and ice coverage as well as temperatures and atmospheric phenomena related to arctic climate change see the National Snow & Ice Data Center in

Boulder, Colorado. Access to data is provided on the web at the *National Snow & Ice Data Center Home Page,* http://www.nsidc.org (accessed January 21, 2013).

[21] Frederic Lassere, "Arctic Shipping Routes: from the Panama Myth to Reality," *International Journal,* (Autumn 2011), 795.

[22] Ibid, 801; Brigham, "Think Again: The Arctic," 73-74.

[23] U.S. Geological Survey, *Circum-Arctic Resource Appraisal: Estimates of Undiscovered Oil and Gas North of the Arctic Circle* (Menlo Park, CA: U.S. Geological Survey, May 2008), 1, http://pubs.usgs.gov/fs/2008/3049/fs2008-3049.pdf (accessed January 21, 2013).

[24] Admiral Robert J. Papp, Jr. "The Emerging Arctic Frontier," *Proceedings* 138, no.2 (February 2012): 2, in Proquest (accessed January 13, 2013).

[25] Kari Roberts, "Jets, Flags, And A New Cold War: Demystifying Russia's Arctic Intentions," *International Journal,* (Autumn 2010), 966-967.

[26] Ibid.

[27] Angela Stent, "US-Russia Relations in the Second Obama Administration," *Survival: Global Politics and Strategy* 54, no. 6 (November 2012): 133, in Taylor and Francis (accessed January 22, 2013).

[28] Hillary Clinton, "Interview with Secretary of State Hillary Clinton," interview by Michele Kelemen, National Public Radio, January 29, 2013, http://www.npr.org/2013/01/29/170615713/interview-with-secretary-of-state-hillary-clinton (accessed March 3, 2013).

[29] Peter Ohotnicky, Braden Hisey, and Jessica Todd, "Improving US Posture in the Arctic," *Joint Force Quarterly,* no.67 (4th Quarter 2012): 58.

[30] Barack Obama, *National Security Strategy,* (Washington, DC: The White House, May 2010), 17.

[31] George W. Bush, *National Security Presidential Directive-66 and Homeland Security Presidential Directive-25: Arctic Region Policy* (Washington, DC: The White House, January 9, 2009), 1.

[32] Hillary Clinton, interviewed by Michele Kelemen, National Public Radio online.

[33] Barack Obama and Leon Panetta, *Sustaining U.S. Global Leadership: Priorities for 21st Century Defense,* (Washington, DC: The Pentagon, January 2012), cover memo; Barack Obama, "Remarks by President Obama to the Australian Parliament," speech, Canberra, *Australia*, 17 November 2011.

[34] Robert M. Gates, *Quadrennial Defense Review,* (Washington, DC: US Department of Defense, February 2010), 11.

[35] U.S. Department of Defense, *Report to Congress on Arctic Operations and the Northwest Passage,* (Washington, DC: U.S. Department of Defense, May 2011), 8-9.

[36] Bush, *NSPD-66*, 3.

[37] Scott G. Borgerson, *The National Interest and the Law of the Sea* (New York: Council on Foreign Relations, May 2009), 28.

[38] *The Arctic Council Home Page*, http://www.arctic-council.org/index.php/en (accessed January 10, 2013).

[39] Barack Obama, *Unified Command Plan,* (Washington, DC: The White House, April 2011), 14.

[40] Ohotnicky et al, "Improving U.S. Posture," 59.

[41] Papp, "The Emerging Arctic Frontier," 16.

[42]U.S. Department of Defense, *Report to Congress*, 14-16.

[43] *The Arctic Council Home Page*, http://www.arctic-council.org/index.php/en (accessed January 10, 2013).

[44] Gates, *Quadrennial Defense Review,* 11.

[45] Ohotnicky et al, "Improving U.S. Posture," 60.

[46] U.S. Department of Defense, *Report to Congress,* 16.

www.ingramcontent.com/pod-product-compliance
Lightning Source LLC
Chambersburg PA
CBHW081546280526
45788CB00010B/3371